The Spirit Guide

Nurturing The Bond
WITH YOUR SPIRITUAL ANIMAL

Dr. Jilesh

Copyright © 2023 by Jilesh Thilakan

Disclaimer: The information provided in this book is for general informational purposes only. The content is based on the concept of spiritual animal guides and their significance in various spiritual traditions. The author and publisher make no representation or warranty regarding the accuracy, efficacy, or outcomes resulting from the practices described in this book.

The reader understands and acknowledges that experiences and interpretations of spiritual animal guides may vary. It is important to exercise personal discernment and respect individual beliefs and cultural traditions. The author and publisher disclaim any liability for any loss or damage incurred by the reader or any third party directly or indirectly as a result of the use or application of the information presented in this book.

The connection with a spiritual animal guide is a personal and intuitive experience. If you have any specific concerns or questions about working with spiritual animal guides, please consult with a qualified spiritual teacher or practitioner.

---

1. https://www.healingoraclewisdom.com/

About the Author

Dr. Jilesh is a renowned and highly rated manifestation expert, spell caster, psychotherapist, life coach, and master of business administration. With extensive experience and expertise in the field, Dr. Jilesh has garnered a reputation as a trusted authority in the realm of manifestation and personal transformation.

As a highly rated manifestation expert and spell caster on Fiverr, Check Global Reviews here - https://www.fiverr.com/jileshthilakan?up_rollout=true[1] Dr.Jilesh has assisted countless individuals in manifesting their desires and achieving their goals. Through his deep understanding of the principles of manifestation, Dr. Jilesh has helped clients tap into their innate power to create their dream reality.

In addition to his work on Fiverr, **Dr. Jilesh has also excelled as a highly rated instructor on Udemy, with more than 30k students** Check his personal development courses here - https://www.udemy.com/user/jilesh-thilakan/ [2]sharing his knowledge and empowering students worldwide to harness the power of manifestation. With a passion for teaching and a commitment to providing valuable insights, Dr. Jilesh has garnered a loyal following of students who have experienced transformation and success under his guidance.

Dr. Jilesh's expertise extends beyond manifestation, as he is also a qualified psychotherapist and life coach. His background in psychology and counselling allows him to provide holistic support to individuals seeking personal growth and transformation. Through his empathetic approach and profound insights, Dr. Jilesh helps clients overcome challenges, break through limiting beliefs, and create lasting positive change in their lives.

Furthermore, Dr. Jilesh holds a master's degree in business administration, which adds a unique perspective to his work. His understanding of business principles and strategies allows him to guide individuals in aligning their personal goals with professional success, creating a harmonious balance between their aspirations and career pursuits.

With a diverse skill set and a genuine passion for helping others, Dr. Jilesh is committed to empowering individuals to unlock their full potential and manifest a life of abundance, fulfilment, and joy. Through his teachings, guidance, and transformative techniques, he aims to inspire and support others on their journey towards manifesting their deepest desires and living their best lives. **For more about Author checkout his Blog-** https://www.healingoraclewisdom.com/

Chapter 1

The Call of the Wild

In the vast tapestry of existence, there exists a subtle thread that connects us to the untamed realms of the wild. It is a call that resonates deep within our souls, beckoning us to venture beyond the boundaries of the known and embrace the mysteries of the natural world. This call of the wild is not merely a whim or a passing fancy; it is a profound invitation to embark on a transformative journey of self-discovery, guided by the enigmatic presence of our spiritual animal.

The call often begins as a gentle whisper, barely audible amidst the cacophony of daily life. But as we open ourselves to the possibility of something greater, the whispers grow louder, more insistent. Signs and synchronicities weave their intricate patterns, subtly nudging us towards a path that leads to the revelation of our spiritual animal. Perhaps it is a chance encounter with a particular animal in the physical world - a fleeting glimpse of a magnificent creature or an encounter that seems to defy logical explanation. Or maybe it is a recurring dream, where a creature of extraordinary beauty and power appears, leaving an indelible impression upon our waking consciousness.

Whatever form it takes, the call of the wild stirs something deep within us - an ancient memory, a primal connection that transcends time and space. It is a call that resonates with the very essence of our being, awakening dormant energies and inviting us to step into a more profound understanding of ourselves and the world around us. As we embark on this journey, it is important to recognize that the call of the wild is not a mere whim or fleeting fascination. It is a profound invitation from the universe - a beckoning to explore the depths of our own nature, to unlock the hidden realms of our psyche, and to embrace the wisdom and guidance of our spiritual animal. The first step in answering this call is to cultivate a sense of openness and receptivity. We must be willing to suspend our disbelief, to let go of preconceived notions, and to approach the journey with a sense of wonder and curiosity. It is through this openness that the signs and synchronicities can reveal themselves, guiding us towards the discovery of our spiritual animal. The call of the wild also requires us to cultivate a deeper connection with nature. In the bustling chaos of modern life, it is all too easy to become disconnected from the natural world - to overlook the intricate beauty that surrounds us and to lose sight of our place within the greater web of life.

Yet, it is within the embrace of nature that the call of the wild finds its most profound resonance. By immersing ourselves in the sights, sounds, and sensations of the natural world, we create fertile ground for the call to take root and flourish.

But answering the call of the wild is not a solitary endeavour. It is a journey that is meant to be shared - a collective exploration of our interconnectedness and shared destiny. As we embark on this path, we may discover kindred spirits who have heard the same call, who are traversing the same untamed landscapes of the soul. Together, we can offer support, guidance, and companionship as we navigate the mysterious terrain that lies before us.

Exploring the Signs and Synchronicities that Lead Us to Our Spiritual Animal

As we heed the call of the wild, embarking on a journey of self-discovery and connection with our spiritual animal, the universe begins to weave a tapestry of signs and synchronicities, guiding us along the path of discovery. These subtle messages, often disguised as ordinary events or occurrences, carry profound meaning and serve as guideposts on our transformative journey. The signs and synchronicities may manifest in various forms, drawing our attention and evoking a sense of intrigue and curiosity. It could be as simple as repeatedly encountering a specific animal in our daily lives - a bird that seems to appear at just the right moment or a particular creature that captures our gaze with its mesmerizing presence. These encounters may occur unexpectedly, in the most unlikely places, yet they resonate deep within us, stirring a sense of familiarity and connection. Dreams, too, hold a powerful realm where the signs and messages of our spiritual animal can emerge. In the realm of dreams, the boundaries between the physical and spiritual worlds blur, and our subconscious mind becomes a conduit for profound insights and guidance.

A dream may feature an animal, vivid and symbolic, carrying with it a message or a lesson meant specifically for us. These dreams often linger in our waking consciousness, leaving an indelible imprint upon our souls, and we find ourselves compelled to explore their deeper significance. The synchronicities that accompany the call of the wild are not mere coincidences; rather, they are the orchestrated whispers of the universe, orchestrating a symphony of guidance and connection. They may manifest as a sequence of numbers that repeat themselves in unexpected places - a specific pattern that seems to follow us wherever we go. These numbers hold a sacred code, a language that transcends the rational and invites us to contemplate their meaning and significance. Other synchronicities may manifest as unexpected encounters with books, articles, or conversations that revolve around the themes and symbolism of our spiritual animal.

It may feel as if the world around us conspires to bring these messages to our attention, gently nudging us towards a deeper exploration and understanding of our unique bond. To uncover the hidden wisdom embedded within these signs and synchronicities, it is essential to cultivate a heightened awareness and attunement to the world around us. This requires us to embrace a state of mindfulness - an openness to the present moment and a willingness to perceive the extraordinary within the ordinary. By quieting the noise of our daily lives and tuning in to the subtle whispers of the universe, we create space for the signs to reveal themselves. Journaling can be a powerful practice to document and reflect upon the signs and synchronicities that unfold in our lives.

By recording these experiences, we begin to discern patterns and themes that emerge, enabling us to gain deeper insights into the messages that our spiritual animal wishes to convey.

The act of journaling itself becomes an act of reverence, a sacred dialogue between ourselves and the divine forces guiding our journey. As we explore the signs and synchronicities that lead us to our spiritual animal, it is essential to approach them with a sense of wonder, curiosity, and trust. Embrace the mystery and allow yourself to be guided by the unfolding journey. Sometimes the signs may be subtle, requiring us to engage in introspection and reflection.

Other times, they may be unmistakable, revealing themselves with clarity and certainty. Trust in the process, for the universe conspires in its infinite wisdom to lead us to the profound connection we seek. Open your heart and mind to the whispers of the universe. Allow the signs and synchronicities to guide your steps, for they are the breadcrumbs that lead you closer to the profound bond with your spiritual animal. Trust in the unseen forces that weave their magic through your life, and embrace the journey of exploration and revelation that awaits.

Delving Deeper into the Specific Signs, Symbols, and Messages Associated with Different Spiritual Animals

The signs associated with spiritual animals can manifest in a myriad of ways, reflecting the diverse and awe-inspiring aspects of the natural world. It could be a specific animal appearing in our dreams, visions, or meditations - a vivid encounter that leaves an indelible mark on our consciousness. Through these encounters, we glimpse into the realm of the spirit, where our spiritual animal imparts profound lessons, guidance, and healing energy. Symbols act as a language of the soul, transcending verbal communication and tapping into the depths of our subconscious.

Each spiritual animal possesses its own set of symbols, which serve as keys to unlocking their messages. These symbols can be found in ancient mythologies, folklore, and cultural representations, carrying universal meanings and archetypal significance. For example, the eagle embodies qualities of strength, freedom, and vision. Its soaring flight represents transcendence and the ability to rise above challenges. The owl, with its wisdom and nocturnal nature, symbolizes intuition, mysticism, and the exploration of the hidden realms of consciousness. The bear, known for its power and wisdom, is associated with grounding, introspection, and healing. By delving into the symbols associated with our spiritual animal, we gain deeper insights into their essence and the aspects of ourselves they reflect and illuminate. The messages conveyed by our spiritual animals can be deciphered through careful observation, introspection, and attunement to our inner wisdom. They may come in the form of repetitive

patterns in our lives, emphasizing particular traits or lessons we need to cultivate.

The spiritual animal may also use synchronicities and external events to communicate messages, orchestrating encounters and circumstances that mirror the teachings and energies they embody. To fully comprehend these signs, symbols, and messages, it is essential to develop a personal relationship with our spiritual animal. Engaging in meditation, contemplation, and connection with nature allows us to establish a deeper connection with our spiritual animal, opening ourselves to their teachings and guidance. By cultivating a receptive state of mind and heart, we create a sacred space for their messages to unfold and resonate within us. Journaling continues to be an invaluable tool on this journey, enabling us to record and reflect upon the signs, symbols, and messages we receive. Through the act of writing, we can explore the nuances of our experiences, uncover patterns, and gain a deeper understanding of the profound lessons our spiritual animal imparts. Additionally, seeking knowledge from ancient wisdom traditions, books, and other resources dedicated to animal symbolism can provide further insights and expand our comprehension of the spiritual animal realm.

As we delve deeper into the specific signs, symbols, and messages associated with different spiritual animals, we embark on a voyage of self-discovery and spiritual growth. Each encounter, each symbol, and each message serves as a stepping stone on our path, guiding us toward greater self-awareness, inner harmony, and alignment with the natural world. Our spiritual animal becomes not just a guide, but a mirror reflecting the hidden aspects of ourselves and illuminating the transformative journey that lies before us.

Chapter 2

The Encounter

In the realm of the spiritual animal, the transformative journey begins with a profound encounter. It is an extraordinary moment, a meeting of souls that transcends the boundaries of the physical world. This chapter explores the significance of the encounter - the sacred meeting point where our lives intersect with the mystical presence of our spiritual animal. The encounter can take various forms, each one unique and deeply personal. For some, it may be a sudden and unexpected sighting - an animal appearing seemingly out of nowhere, capturing our attention with its commanding presence. It could be a majestic eagle soaring across the sky, a graceful deer gracefully crossing our path, or a wise owl perched on a branch, fixing its penetrating gaze upon us.

In that instant, our hearts recognize the significance of the encounter, and a sense of awe and reverence washes over us. Other encounters may come in the form of dreams or visions. As we surrender to the realm of sleep, the boundaries between the physical and the spiritual dissolve, allowing our spiritual animal to visit us in the depths of our subconscious. In these dreams, we experience a profound connection - a meeting of spirits that transcends time and space. The encounter leaves an imprint upon our waking consciousness, carrying a profound sense of guidance and purpose.

In some cases, the encounter may even manifest as an energetic presence - an invisible force that we feel rather than see. We might sense the essence of our spiritual animal during meditation or moments of solitude in nature. It could be a tingling sensation, a gentle whisper in the breeze, or an inexplicable feeling of being watched and protected. These encounters remind us of the unseen realms that intertwine with our daily lives, revealing the interconnectedness of all beings. The encounter with our spiritual animal is not a chance happening; it is a divine orchestration - an invitation from the universe to embark on a profound journey of self-discovery and growth. It is a recognition of the sacred bond that exists between us and our spiritual animal - a bond that transcends the limitations of language and logic. When we encounter our spiritual animal, it is essential to approach the meeting with reverence, humility, and an open heart.

The encounter carries a potent energy - a force that has the power to awaken dormant aspects of our being and ignite the flame of transformation within us. It is an opportunity to glimpse into the depths of our own souls, to explore the uncharted territories of our inner landscape, and to connect with the wisdom and guidance of our spiritual animal. To deepen our understanding of the encounter, it is beneficial to engage in practices that foster connection and receptivity. Meditation, for instance, allows us to quiet the mind and attune ourselves to the subtle frequencies of the spiritual realm.

By entering a state of stillness, we create a sacred space for our spiritual animal to make its presence known, to impart its teachings, and to offer guidance on our path. Spending time in nature also opens the channels of communication with our spiritual animal. The natural world is a tapestry of interconnectedness, and by immersing ourselves in its embrace, we align ourselves with the rhythms and energies that underpin our existence. It is in these moments of communion with nature that our spiritual animal can reveal itself, guiding us through its manifestations and synchronicities. In the encounter, we are invited to observe, to listen, and to learn. Our spiritual animal communicates through subtle cues and symbolic gestures, inviting us to interpret the messages embedded within. Paying attention to the behaviour, characteristics, and unique qualities of our spiritual animal allows us to gain insights into our own strengths, challenges, and potentials. By aligning ourselves with its teachings, we can navigate the complexities of life with greater wisdom and grace.

The encounter is not a one-time event; it marks the beginning of an ongoing relationship with our spiritual animal. It is a bond that deepens and evolves over time, as we continue to honour and nurture the connection. Through rituals, offerings, and acts of gratitude, we can express our reverence for our spiritual animal and invite its continued presence in our lives. As we cultivate this relationship, we realize that our spiritual animal is not merely an external guide but a reflection of our own innate wisdom and power.

Chapter 3

The Essence Within

Within the realm of our spiritual animal lies a sacred essence - a profound reflection of our own inner being. This chapter explores the depths of this essence, guiding us to explore the hidden aspects of ourselves that are illuminated through our connection with our spiritual animal. By diving into the essence within, we embark on a journey of self-discovery, transformation, and profound alignment with our true nature. Our spiritual animal serves as a mirror, reflecting the qualities, strengths, and challenges that reside within us. Its essence resonates with our own, calling forth aspects of ourselves that may have remained dormant or unrecognized. As we delve into this profound connection, we uncover the layers of our being, shedding light on the intricacies of our soul. Each spiritual animal carries its unique essence - an embodiment of virtues, characteristics, and energies that hold deep significance. For example, the lion represents courage, leadership, and strength. Its essence embodies the qualities of bravery, confidence, and assertiveness. The gentle deer symbolizes grace, sensitivity, and intuition. By connecting with its essence, we tap into our own capacity for empathy, gentleness, and attunement to the natural world.

Exploring the essence within begins with self-reflection and introspection. It requires a willingness to embark on an inner journey, peering into the depths of our own consciousness and embracing the aspects of ourselves that may have been neglected or overlooked. Through practices such as meditation, journaling, and contemplation, we create a sacred space to connect with the essence of our spiritual animal and explore its resonance within our own being.In the stillness of meditation, we can delve into the depths of our soul and listen to the whispers of our spiritual animal's essence. By quieting the mind and opening our hearts, we invite its presence to guide us, revealing the qualities and attributes that are calling for our attention and nurturing. Through meditation, we cultivate a deeper understanding of ourselves, our desires, and our purpose. Journaling serves as a powerful tool to explore the essence within. By putting pen to paper, we allow our thoughts and emotions to flow freely, capturing the insights and revelations that arise during our journey of self-discovery. Through journaling, we gain clarity, notice patterns, and uncover the hidden treasures of our inner landscape.

It is a sacred dialogue between ourselves and the essence of our spiritual animal, a profound exchange that deepens our connection and brings forth profound wisdom. As we explore the essence within, we may encounter aspects of ourselves that challenge or stretch our comfort zones. Our spiritual animal acts as a gentle guide, urging us to embrace the full spectrum of our being - the light and the shadow. By embracing both our strengths and weaknesses,

we attain a state of wholeness and integration, aligning with the essence within and embodying the transformative power it holds. The essence within also invites us to embody the qualities and energies of our spiritual animal in our daily lives. It is an invitation to step into our authenticity, expressing our unique essence and honouring the gifts that we carry within. When we align ourselves with the essence of our spiritual animal, we tap into a wellspring of inspiration, creativity, and personal power. The essence within is not static - it is a dynamic force that evolves and expands as we grow on our spiritual journey. As we deepen our connection with our spiritual animal, we gain a deeper understanding of our own essence and its connection to the greater tapestry of life.

We recognize that we are part of a web of interconnectedness - a sacred dance where our individual essence contributes to the harmony and balance of the whole. In the chapters to come, we will continue to explore the essence within, delving into the specific qualities, energies, and teachings of various spiritual animals. We will navigate the intricacies of our own being, recognizing the profound resonance that exists between ourselves and our spiritual animal. By embracing the essence within, we embark on a transformative path of self-discovery, growth, and the realization of our true potential.

Chapter 4

Building Trust and Reciprocity

In the sacred bond with our spiritual animal, trust and reciprocity form the foundation upon which our connection thrives. This chapter explores the significance of building trust and cultivating a reciprocal relationship with our spiritual animal. As we delve into the depths of this profound connection, we learn to honour, respect, and engage in a mutual exchange that nourishes our souls and amplifies the transformative power of the bond. Trust is the cornerstone of any meaningful relationship, and our connection with our spiritual animal is no exception. Trusting in the unseen, the mystical, and the unknown, we open ourselves to the wisdom and guidance of our spiritual animal. It is through trust that we surrender to the flow of the journey, allowing ourselves to be guided by the unseen forces that weave their magic through our lives.

Building trust begins with attuning ourselves to the subtle cues, messages, and synchronicities that our spiritual animal presents. It is a process of deepening our intuition and learning to decipher the language of the spirit. As we navigate the ebb and flow of this connection, we recognize the inherent trustworthiness of our spiritual animal, understanding that its presence and guidance are rooted in love and divine guidance. To build trust, it is essential to approach our encounters with patience, respect, and an open heart. We honour the boundaries and needs of our spiritual animal, allowing it to reveal itself to us in its own time and in its own way. Trust is nurtured through consistent presence, acknowledging and valuing the connection even in the quiet moments when our spiritual animal seems distant. It is a testament to our faith and commitment to the bond we share.

Reciprocity is the dynamic dance of give and take, a sacred exchange that fuels the growth and nourishment of our connection. It is the act of honouring and reciprocating the gifts, teachings, and energy that our spiritual animal bestows upon us. Just as we seek guidance and support from our spiritual animal, we too have the opportunity to contribute to its well-being and the well-being of the natural world. Reciprocity involves showing gratitude and expressing our appreciation for the presence and teachings of our spiritual animal. Through rituals, offerings, and acts of reverence, we acknowledge the sacredness of the bond and honour the reciprocal nature of the relationship. Whether it is leaving an offering in nature, performing a ceremony in honour of our spiritual animal, or simply expressing heartfelt gratitude, each act becomes a thread that weaves the tapestry of reciprocity.

It is through reciprocity that we deepen our connection with our spiritual animal. By actively engaging in a reciprocal relationship, we become co-creators in the transformative journey we embark upon. We listen to the messages, lessons, and guidance that our spiritual animal imparts and integrate them into our lives. In turn, we offer our love, intention, and energy to support and uplift our spiritual animal on its own evolutionary path. Reciprocity also extends to our relationship with the natural world. Our spiritual animal serves as a bridge, connecting us to the web of life and reminding us of our interconnectedness with all beings. By honouring and caring for the Earth, we demonstrate our commitment to reciprocity and contribute to the greater balance and harmony of the planet.

Building trust and cultivating reciprocity require a deep sense of presence and attunement. It is a continuous process of deepening our awareness, aligning with the rhythms of nature, and listening to the subtle whispers of our spiritual animal. Through meditation, contemplation, and communion with nature, we create a sacred space for the bond to flourish and expand.

Chapter 5

Guidance on the Journey

On the profound path of the spiritual animal, guidance becomes an invaluable companion, illuminating our way and offering support as we navigate the twists and turns of our personal journey. This chapter explores the significance of guidance and the various forms it takes, empowering us to embrace the wisdom and direction that our spiritual animal provides. With its guidance, we find solace, clarity, and a deep sense of purpose on our transformative journey. Guidance comes in myriad forms, each one uniquely tailored to our individual needs and circumstances. One of the most profound ways our spiritual animal offers guidance is through signs and symbols. These sacred messages are embedded in the fabric of our daily lives, waiting to be deciphered and embraced. It could be a recurring dream, a meaningful encounter with a specific animal, or a series of synchronistic events that capture our attention.

As we attune ourselves to the subtle language of our spiritual animal, we uncover the guidance and insights that lie within these signs and symbols, unveiling a deeper understanding of ourselves and the path we tread. The guidance of our spiritual animal also emerges through our intuition - a powerful inner compass that guides us toward our highest good. As we deepen our connection with our spiritual animal, we cultivate a heightened sensitivity to the subtle energies and messages that flow through our being. By trusting our intuition, we navigate the complexities of life with greater clarity, making choices that align with our authentic selves and serve our soul's purpose. Our spiritual animal serves as a gentle guide, nudging us toward the path that resonates most deeply with our hearts. Meditation is a potent practice that opens the gateway to receiving guidance from our spiritual animal. In the stillness of meditation, we create a sacred space to connect with the wisdom and presence of our spiritual animal. By quieting the mind and opening our hearts, we invite its guidance to flow through us, gaining insights and clarity that transcend the limitations of the rational mind. Meditation becomes a sacred dialogue - a profound exchange of energy and wisdom that deepens our connection and enriches our journey.

Nature itself serves as a powerful source of guidance on our spiritual path. As we immerse ourselves in the natural world, we attune ourselves to its rhythms, cycles, and wisdom. Our spiritual animal reveals itself through the beauty of the landscape, the songs of the birds, and the dance of the elements. By observing and communing with nature, we receive guidance and messages that align with

our spiritual growth and provide solace and inspiration during times of uncertainty.

Nature becomes a living testament to the interconnectedness of all beings and a reminder of the wisdom that resides within us and around us. The guidance of our spiritual animal is not limited to external signs and messages. It also manifests through the depths of our own being. Through introspection and self-reflection, we tap into the wellspring of wisdom that lies within our souls. Our spiritual animal acts as a catalyst, awakening dormant aspects of our being, and guiding us toward our true nature. By embracing the lessons and qualities embodied by our spiritual animal, we unlock our own potential and embark on a journey of self-discovery and transformation.

Rituals and ceremonies offer a powerful means of invoking the guidance of our spiritual animal. Through sacred practices, we create a space to honour and commune with the essence of our spiritual animal. Whether it is through offerings, prayers, or sacred dances, rituals serve as a bridge that connects us to the unseen realms, amplifying the guidance and presence of our spiritual animal. These acts of devotion become a portal through which we receive clarity, direction, and a deep sense of connection. The guidance of our spiritual animal is not always linear or predictable. It may come in flashes of insight, whispers in the wind, or gentle nudges that redirect our path. It requires us to remain open and receptive, trusting in the wisdom and divine timing of our spiritual animal. By surrendering to the flow of guidance, we embrace the unknown and allow ourselves to be guided toward our highest potential.

Chapter 6

<u>Deepening the Connection</u>

The bond with our spiritual animal is a sacred tapestry woven with threads of love, trust, and profound connection. In this chapter, we explore the depths of this connection, delving into practices and experiences that enable us to deepen our relationship with our spiritual animal. As we dive into the depths of this profound connection, we discover new dimensions of ourselves, the spiritual realms, and the transformative power that lies within. To deepen our connection with our spiritual animal, it is essential to cultivate a state of presence and attunement. This begins with carving out sacred moments of stillness and solitude, allowing ourselves to fully immerse in the energy and essence of our spiritual animal. By quieting the external noise and turning our attention inward, we create a fertile ground for the blossoming of our connection. In this space of inner stillness, we can hear the whispers of our spiritual animal and feel its presence with heightened sensitivity.

One powerful practice for deepening the connection is active imagination. Through the power of visualization and creative exploration, we can engage in a dialogue with our spiritual animal, allowing it to reveal itself in vivid detail. By immersing ourselves in this inner landscape, we establish a profound connection that transcends the limitations of the physical world. Through active imagination, we tap into the wisdom, guidance, and healing energy of our spiritual animal, accessing profound insights and transformative experiences.

Dreamwork also serves as a potent tool for deepening the connection. Our dreams are a portal to the subconscious realms, where our spiritual animal can communicate with us in symbolic and profound ways. By keeping a dream journal and actively engaging with our dream experiences, we unravel the hidden messages, teachings, and guidance embedded within our dreams. Through dreamwork, we forge a deeper relationship with our spiritual animal, receiving its wisdom and guidance even as we slumber.

The practice of shamanic journeying offers a profound means of deepening the connection with our spiritual animal. Through rhythmic drumming or other trance-inducing techniques, we enter an altered state of consciousness, transcending the boundaries of ordinary reality. In this expanded state, we can embark on journeys to meet and commune with our spiritual animal in the realms beyond the physical. These journeys provide opportunities for direct communication, healing, and the exploration of the spiritual realms. By engaging in shamanic journeying, we enter into a sacred dialogue with our spiritual animal, deepening our connection and expanding our understanding of ourselves and the mysteries of existence. Nature itself becomes a sacred teacher and partner in deepening the connection.

By spending time in the natural world, we attune ourselves to the rhythms, cycles, and energies that permeate all of creation. In the embrace of nature, we find solace, inspiration, and a profound sense of connection with our spiritual animal. Whether it is through hiking in the mountains, sitting by a flowing river, or simply resting under a tree, nature invites us to witness the beauty and wisdom of our spiritual animal in its natural habitat. By immersing ourselves in nature, we create a harmonious resonance that strengthens our bond and deepens our understanding of the interconnectedness of all life. Prayer and sacred rituals serve as powerful vehicles for deepening our connection with our spiritual animal. By creating sacred space, invoking our spiritual animal with reverence and gratitude, and engaging in acts of devotion, we cultivate a container of sacred energy that amplifies the presence and guidance of our spiritual animal.

These rituals become portals of connection, merging the physical and spiritual realms, and facilitating a deeper communion with our spiritual animal. Journaling continues to be a valuable practice for deepening the connection. By capturing our thoughts, experiences, and insights on paper, we create a tangible record of our journey and the profound moments shared with our spiritual animal. Journaling allows us to reflect, process, and integrate the wisdom and teachings received from our spiritual animal. It serves as a personal archive of our spiritual evolution, documenting the growth and transformation that unfold along the path.

Unveiling Your Spiritual Animal: Discover Your Archetypal Connection

Instructions: Select the option that best resonates with you for each question. Keep track of your answers to determine your spiritual animal archetype at the end.

Which quality resonates with you the most?

a) Strength and resilience

b) Freedom and curiosity

c) Passion and courage

d) Intuition and adaptability

What natural element captivates you?

a) Earth (mountains, forests)

b) Air (skies, open spaces)

c) Fire (desert, flames)

d) Water (oceans, rivers)

How do you handle challenges?

a) With patience and stability

b) By seeking new perspectives

c) With bold action and determination

d) Trusting your intuition and going with the flow

What role do relationships play in your life?

a) Loyalty and nurturing support

b) Independence and open-mindedness

c) Empowerment and protection

d) Intuition and emotional connection

Which word resonates with your spiritual connection?

a) Grounding

b) Exploration

c) Empowerment

d) Intuition

How do you find inspiration and guidance?

a) Connecting with nature

b) Engaging in creative pursuits

c) Pursuing passionate endeavours

d) Reflecting and listening to your inner voice

Which animal archetype captivates you the most?

a) Bear: Strength and introspection

b) Owl: Wisdom and intuition

c) Lion: Courage and leadership

d) Dolphin: Joy and emotional intelligence

What aspect of yourself would you like to enhance?

a) Grounding and stability

b) Freedom and exploration

c) Passion and confidence

d) Intuition and self-awareness

Now, calculate your answers and discover your spiritual animal archetype based on the highest letter frequencies:

Mostly A's: Your spiritual animal archetype is connected to the Earth element, such as a bear or a turtle.

Mostly B's: Your spiritual animal archetype is connected to the Air element, such as an owl or a butterfly.

Mostly C's: Your spiritual animal archetype is connected to the Fire element, such as a lion or a phoenix.

Mostly D's: Your spiritual animal archetype is connected to the Water element, such as a dolphin or a whale.

Some specific qualities, energies, and teachings associated with various spiritual animals:

Bear:

Qualities: Strength, resilience, and introspection.

Energies: Grounding, stability, and protection.

Teachings: Embrace solitude for self-reflection, draw upon inner strength during challenges, and seek wisdom in hibernation periods.

Owl:

Qualities: Wisdom, intuition, and clarity.

Energies: Insight, perception, and spiritual guidance.

Teachings: Trust your intuition, embrace the power of observation, and seek wisdom in the shadows of life.

Lion:

Qualities: Courage, leadership, and personal power.

Energies: Strength, confidence, and assertiveness.

Teachings: Embrace your inner strength, take decisive action, and lead with compassion and dignity.

Dolphin:

Qualities: Joy, harmony, and emotional intelligence.

Energies: Playfulness, communication, and empathy.

Teachings: Cultivate joy in your life, embrace the power of connection, and navigate emotional depths with grace and compassion.

Eagle:

Qualities: Vision, clarity, and spiritual insight.

Energies: Awareness, perspective, and transcendence.

Teachings: Rise above challenges, gain a broader perspective on life, and trust your higher vision and intuition.

Turtle:

Qualities: Wisdom, patience, and longevity.

Energies: Grounding, protection, and perseverance.

Teachings: Cultivate patience in all aspects of life, honour the importance of grounding and stability, and trust in the divine timing of events.

Butterfly:

Qualities: Transformation, rebirth, and spiritual growth.

Energies: Freedom, lightness, and beauty.

Teachings: Embrace change and transformation, honour the process of growth, and find the beauty in life's transitions.

Wolf:

Qualities: Loyalty, intuition, and teamwork.

Energies: Guardianship, instincts, and community.

Teachings: Cultivate strong bonds and loyalty in relationships, trust your instincts and intuition, and work together for the greater good.

Snake:

Qualities: Transformation, rebirth, and healing.

Energies: Renewal, shedding of old patterns, and transformation.

Teachings: Embrace change and personal growth, release what no longer serves you, and harness the power of healing and regeneration.

Elephant:

Qualities: Strength, wisdom, and spiritual connection.

Energies: Protection, memory, and family bonds.

Teachings: Honour ancestral wisdom, embrace the strength within you, and value the importance of community and nurturing relationships.

Deer:

Qualities: Gentleness, grace, and connection with nature.

Energies: Sensitivity, intuition, and harmony.

Teachings: Find peace and serenity in nature, trust your instincts, and move through life with grace and gentleness.

Fox:

Qualities: Cunning, adaptability, and quick thinking.

Energies: Cleverness, agility, and camouflage.

Teachings: Embrace adaptability and resourcefulness, trust your instincts, and navigate through challenges with wit and cleverness.

Horse:

Qualities: Freedom, power, and overcoming obstacles.

Energies: Strength, endurance, and connection with the natural world.

Teachings: Embrace freedom in all aspects of life, face challenges head-on, and cultivate a deep connection with your inner strength and intuition.

Dragonfly:

Qualities: Change, adaptability, and the power of light.

Energies: Transformation, agility, and the ability to see beyond illusion.

Teachings: Embrace personal growth and transformation, trust in the process of change, and see through illusions to find deeper truths.

Whale:

Qualities: Intuition, emotional depth, and spiritual communication.

Energies: Wisdom, introspection, and connection with the subconscious.

Teachings: Dive deep into your emotions and intuition, communicate your truth, and listen to the wisdom within the depths of your being.

Tiger:

Qualities: Strength, courage, and determination.

Energies: Power, stealth, and independence.

Teachings: Embrace your personal power, face challenges with courage, and embody strength and determination in all aspects of life.

Hummingbird:

Qualities: Joy, adaptability, and lightness of being.

Energies: Playfulness, curiosity, and swift action.

Teachings: Embrace the sweetness of life, find joy in the present moment, and navigate through life's challenges with grace and agility.

Peacock:

Qualities: Beauty, confidence, and self-expression.

Energies: Vibrancy, extravagance, and spiritual awakening.

Teachings: Embrace your unique qualities, express yourself authentically, and radiate your inner beauty and confidence.

Rabbit:

Qualities: Fertility, abundance, and sensitivity.

Energies: Alertness, agility, and gentleness.

Teachings: Trust your instincts, navigate through life with sensitivity and awareness, and embrace the cycles of abundance and growth.

Falcon:

Qualities: Focus, precision, and visionary abilities.

Energies: Clarity, speed, and heightened awareness.

Teachings: Develop keen observation skills, trust your visions and insights, and swiftly act upon your goals and aspirations.

Swan:

Qualities: Grace, beauty, and inner transformation.

Energies: Elegance, purity, and spiritual evolution.

Teachings: Embrace inner transformation, find beauty in all aspects of life, and cultivate grace and harmony in your relationships.

Bee:

Qualities: Hard work, community, and fertility.

Energies: Cooperation, diligence, and abundance.

Teachings: Work harmoniously in a community, value the importance of dedication and productivity, and enjoy the fruits of your labour.

Squirrel:

Qualities: Resourcefulness, preparation, and agility.

Energies: Gathering, adaptability, and conservation.

Teachings: Be resourceful in achieving your goals, prepare for the future, and adapt to changes with nimbleness and quick thinking.

Leopard:

Qualities: Strength, agility, and stealth.

Energies: Confidence, independence, and the power of observation.

Teachings: Embrace your personal strength and agility, trust your instincts, and become aware of your surroundings to navigate life's challenges.

Koala:

Qualities: Serenity, relaxation, and nurturing.

Energies: Calmness, gentleness, and connection with nature.

Teachings: Find peace and tranquillity in simple moments, prioritize self-care and nurturing, and honour your connection with the natural world.

Shark:

Qualities: Power, focus, and adaptability.

Energies: Tenacity, survival instincts, and leadership.

Teachings: Harness your personal power, stay focused on your goals, and adapt to new environments and situations with resilience.

Crow:

Qualities: Intelligence, intuition, and magic.

Energies: Mysticism, transformation, and communication.

Teachings: Trust your intuition, embrace the mystical aspects of life, and use your voice to communicate your truth and wisdom.

Gorilla:

Qualities: Strength, protection, and family bonds.

Energies: Leadership, gentleness, and wisdom.

Teachings: Cultivate strong family and community connections, embody gentle strength, and utilize your wisdom to lead and protect others.

Buffalo:

Qualities: Abundance, gratitude, and grounded ness.

Energies: Endurance, stability, and sacredness.

Teachings: Appreciate the abundance in your life, remain grounded in times of change, and honour the sacredness of all living beings.

Octopus:

Qualities: Adaptability, intelligence, and mystery.

Energies: Flexibility, camouflage, and transformative abilities.

Teachings: Embrace change with ease, tap into your intelligence and problem-solving skills, and explore the depths of your emotions and intuition.

Zebra:

Qualities: Individuality, balance, and uniqueness.

Energies: Harmony, strength, and self-expression.

Teachings: Embrace your individuality, find balance between opposing forces, and express yourself authentically.

Giraffe:

Qualities: Vision, grace, and reaching new heights.

Energies: Intuition, elegance, and adaptability.

Teachings: Trust your inner vision, cultivate grace in your movements, and adapt to new environments with ease.

Lizard:

Qualities: Regeneration, adaptability, and intuition.

Energies: Patience, transformation, and the ability to shed the past.

Teachings: Embrace personal transformation, trust your instincts, and have patience during periods of growth and change.

Kangaroo:

Qualities: Balance, strength, and nurturing.

Energies: Protection, agility, and maternal instincts.

Teachings: Find balance between work and play, tap into your inner strength, and nurture your relationships and dreams.

Otter:

Qualities: Playfulness, joy, and social connection.

Energies: Cooperation, adaptability, and curiosity.

Teachings: Embrace a light-hearted approach to life, foster harmonious relationships, and stay curious and open to new experiences.

Raccoon:

Qualities: Cleverness, resourcefulness, and adaptability.

Energies: Stealth, curiosity, and problem-solving abilities.

Teachings: Tap into your resourcefulness, seek solutions in unconventional ways, and embrace adaptability in different situations.

Hawk:

Qualities: Vision, focus, and perspective.

Energies: Awareness, clarity, and spiritual guidance.

Teachings: Observe situations from a higher perspective, trust your intuition, and harness the power of keen observation.

Remember, the qualities, energies, and teachings associated with spiritual animals can vary across different cultures and individual interpretations. Use these insights as a starting point for deeper exploration and connect with the energies of these animals in your own personal experiences to gain a more profound understanding of their unique teachings in your life.

Chapter 7

Healing and Transformation

Within the sacred bond with our spiritual animal lies the power of healing and transformation. In this chapter, we explore the profound role that our spiritual animal plays in facilitating our personal growth, healing, and spiritual evolution. As we embrace the transformative energies of this connection, we embark on a journey of self-discovery, inner healing, and the emergence of our truest selves. Our spiritual animal serves as a guide and catalyst for healing, offering us profound insights into our patterns, wounds, and areas in need of transformation. It mirrors aspects of ourselves that require attention and invites us to embark on a journey of self-reflection and inner healing. By attuning ourselves to the lessons and wisdom of our spiritual animal, we unlock the potential for deep transformation and spiritual evolution.

The healing power of our spiritual animal extends to all levels of our being -physical, emotional, mental, and spiritual. On the physical level, the presence and energy of our spiritual animal can support our overall well-being and vitality. Its essence may offer us specific healing properties, guiding us towards practices, remedies, or lifestyle changes that contribute to our physical health and balance. Emotionally, our spiritual animal offers solace and support during times of emotional turbulence or trauma. Its presence can provide a sense of comfort, reassurance, and unconditional love. Through the connection with our spiritual animal, we learn to navigate our emotions with greater awareness and compassion, allowing for the release of emotional blockages and the restoration of emotional harmony.

On the mental level, our spiritual animal stimulates our intellectual curiosity, creativity, and expanded awareness. It inspires us to explore new perspectives, challenge limiting beliefs, and embrace a broader understanding of ourselves and the world. By engaging with the teachings and guidance of our spiritual animal, we foster mental clarity, open-mindedness, and a deeper connection with the universal wisdom that flows through us. At the spiritual level, our spiritual animal acts as a bridge between the physical and spiritual realms, guiding us towards a deeper connection with our higher self and the divine. It assists us in unlocking our innate spiritual gifts, expanding our consciousness, and aligning with our soul's purpose. Through the healing and transformation facilitated by our spiritual animal, we awaken to our spiritual potential and embrace our role as co-creators of our reality. The transformative journey with our spiritual animal often involves the process of shadow work - a courageous exploration of our deepest fears, traumas, and unconscious patterns.

Our spiritual animal shines a light on these aspects, inviting us to acknowledge, integrate, and heal them. It supports us in reclaiming our wholeness, embracing our shadow with compassion and acceptance, and stepping into our authentic power. Various practices and rituals can support the healing and transformational process with our spiritual animal. Meditation, energy healing, and breath work enable us to access the subtle energies and guidance of our spiritual animal, facilitating profound shifts and healing on a cellular level. Visualization exercises, guided journeys, and sacred ceremonies offer opportunities to connect with the transformative energies of our spiritual animal and invoke its healing presence. Engaging in creative expression, such as art, music, or dance, allows us to channel the transformative energy of our spiritual animal into tangible form. Through these creative outlets, we give voice to our emotions, thoughts, and experiences, allowing for catharsis, self-expression, and the integration of the healing energies received from our spiritual animal.

Throughout the healing and transformational journey, it is crucial to cultivate self-care, self-compassion, and self-love. By nurturing ourselves on all levels - physically, emotionally, mentally, and spiritually - we create a supportive foundation for healing and growth. Our spiritual animal acts as a steadfast companion on this journey, offering guidance, comfort, and unconditional love as we navigate the depths of our inner landscape.

Chapter 8

Guardians of Nature

In the intricate tapestry of existence, our spiritual animals emerge as guardians of nature, embodying the wisdom, harmony, and interconnectedness of the natural world. In this chapter, we explore the profound role our spiritual animals play as stewards of the Earth and how we can cultivate a deeper reverence and partnership with the natural world through their guidance. Our spiritual animals act as bridges between humanity and the natural realm, offering us a direct connection to the wisdom and energies of the Earth. They teach us to honour and respect the sacredness of all living beings, reminding us of our inherent role as caretakers and protectors of the planet. Through their presence and teachings, we learn to embrace sustainable practices, ecological awareness, and a deep appreciation for the beauty and abundance of the Earth.

As guardians of nature, our spiritual animals invite us to immerse ourselves in the natural world and forge a profound relationship with its elements. They beckon us to listen to the whispering of the wind, to witness the dance of the trees, and to feel the pulse of the Earth beneath our feet. Through these experiences, we develop a reverence for the Earth's intricate ecosystems, recognizing the interconnectedness of all life forms and the impact of our actions upon the delicate balance of nature. Our spiritual animals guide us to engage in sustainable living practices that honour the Earth's resources. They inspire us to reduce our carbon footprint, embrace renewable energy sources, and support conservation efforts. By aligning our actions with the wisdom of our spiritual animal, we become conscious custodians of the Earth, actively working to preserve its beauty and biodiversity for future generations.

One way to deepen our connection with the natural world is through nature-based rituals and ceremonies guided by our spiritual animal. These sacred practices allow us to engage in a dialogue of reciprocity with the Earth, expressing gratitude for its gifts and seeking its guidance and blessings. Through offerings, prayers, and intentional acts of stewardship, we form a symbiotic relationship with nature, acknowledging our interdependence and nurturing a sense of harmony and balance. Our spiritual animals also inspire us to reconnect with the ancient wisdom and traditions of indigenous cultures that have long revered and honoured the Earth. They teach us the importance of indigenous knowledge, sustainable farming practices, and herbal medicine.

By honouring and learning from indigenous wisdom, we gain a deeper understanding of our role as guardians of nature and become advocates for preserving and respecting indigenous cultures and their sacred relationship with the Earth.

Through the guidance of our spiritual animal, we are called to be mindful consumers, making conscious choices that minimize harm to the environment. They encourage us to support ethical and eco-friendly businesses, to reduce waste, and to embrace sustainable alternatives in our daily lives. By aligning our consumption habits with the teachings of our spiritual animal, we contribute to the collective effort of healing and safeguarding the Earth. The call to be guardians of nature extends beyond individual actions. Our spiritual animals inspire us to join forces with like-minded individuals and organizations dedicated to environmental conservation and activism. They guide us to lend our voices, skills, and resources to initiatives that promote ecological awareness, wildlife protection, and the preservation of natural habitats. By coming together in collective action, we amplify our impact and create a powerful force for positive change.

As we deepen our partnership with our spiritual animal and embrace our role as guardians of nature, we experience a profound sense of interconnectedness and harmony. We recognize that the well-being of the Earth is intricately tied to our own well-being and that of future generations. Through our spiritual animal, we awaken to the inherent wisdom, love, and reverence that reside within us, enabling us to protect and honour the Earth as conscious custodians.

Chapter 9

The Collective Consciousness

In the vast tapestry of existence, our spiritual animals serve as conduits to the collective consciousness, linking us to the wisdom, energies, and experiences of all beings. In this chapter, we explore the profound connection between our spiritual animals and the collective consciousness, and how we can tap into this universal field of knowledge and transformation. The collective consciousness represents the shared pool of wisdom, insights, and experiences that transcends individuality and encompasses the entirety of humanity and beyond. It is a vast repository of knowledge, shaped by the thoughts, emotions, and actions of all beings throughout time. Our spiritual animals act as gateways to this collective consciousness, allowing us to access its boundless depths and tap into the infinite wisdom it holds. Through our spiritual animals, we are invited to expand our awareness beyond the limitations of the individual self and connect with the broader tapestry of consciousness. They serve as guides, mentors, and facilitators, helping us navigate the currents of the collective consciousness and access the transformative energies that reside within it. One way we can tap into the collective consciousness is through meditation and contemplative practices. By quieting the mind and opening ourselves to the field of universal consciousness, we create a receptive space for insights, guidance, and intuitive knowing to arise. Our spiritual animals act as companions on this inner journey, guiding us to the depths of collective wisdom and assisting us in translating these insights into practical understanding.

Dreams also offer a gateway to the collective consciousness. As we sleep, our spiritual animals can facilitate connections with the dreamscape, where the boundaries of time, space, and individual identity dissolve. In the realm of dreams, we may receive symbols, messages, and encounters that reflect the collective experiences and energies of humanity. By paying attention to our dreams and engaging in dreamwork practices, we can unravel the layers of meaning embedded within these messages and tap into the collective wisdom they carry.

Synchronicities, or meaningful coincidences, are another manifestation of the interplay between our spiritual animals and the collective consciousness. They are like threads woven into the fabric of our lives, connecting us with the underlying patterns and interconnectedness of the universe. Through synchronicities, our spiritual animals guide us toward significant encounters, opportunities, and experiences that align with our soul's journey.

By recognizing and embracing these synchronistic events, we deepen our connection with the collective consciousness and navigate the currents of life with greater clarity and purpose. Engaging in rituals and ceremonies that honour the collective consciousness is another way to access its transformative power. By coming together in sacred space, we create a collective intention that reverberates through the web of consciousness, amplifying our individual and collective energies. Through these rituals, guided by our spiritual animals, we connect with the ancient wisdom of our ancestors, the collective healing energies, and the shared dreams of humanity.

In these sacred gatherings, we weave our intentions and energies into the fabric of the collective consciousness, co-creating a more compassionate, harmonious, and awakened world. Our spiritual animals also inspire us to engage in acts of service and contribute to the well-being of the collective. They remind us of our interconnectedness and the impact our thoughts, words, and actions have on the greater whole. By aligning ourselves with the values and energies of our spiritual animals, we become catalysts for positive change and agents of transformation in the world. Whether through acts of kindness, social activism, or sharing our unique gifts and talents, we contribute to the collective consciousness and help shape a more conscious and compassionate society. Through our deepened connection with the collective consciousness, we become aware of the interplay between our individual journeys and the broader tapestry of human experience. We recognize that our personal growth, healing, and transformation are interconnected with the evolution of the collective. As we align ourselves with the wisdom and energies of our spiritual animals, we actively participate in the awakening of the collective consciousness and contribute to the co-creation of a more enlightened and harmonious world.

Chapter 10

<u>Embracing the Shadow</u>

Within the depths of our being resides the shadow - a realm of unconscious patterns, repressed emotions, and hidden aspects of ourselves that often elicit fear and discomfort. In this chapter, we explore the transformative power of embracing the shadow with the guidance of our spiritual animals. By shining a light on these obscured parts of ourselves, we uncover profound insights, healing, and integration. Our spiritual animals serve as compassionate allies as we embark on the journey of exploring our shadow. They encourage us to face our fears, confront our past traumas, and acknowledge the aspects of ourselves that we have disowned or rejected. By embracing the shadow, we create the space for profound growth, self-acceptance, and the emergence of our authentic selves. The shadow represents the aspects of ourselves that we deem unacceptable, unworthy, or shameful. It encompasses our deepest fears, suppressed emotions, and the parts of us that have been rejected by societal conditioning or personal judgments. These aspects often hold valuable wisdom and gifts that, once integrated, contribute to our wholeness and evolution. Through the guidance of our spiritual animals, we embark on a process of shadow work - a courageous exploration of our hidden depths. We delve into the shadows, shining a light on the aspects we have long avoided or denied. With the support of our spiritual animals, we learn to embrace these aspects with compassion, understanding, and self-love.

Shadow work involves self-reflection, introspection, and a willingness to confront uncomfortable truths. It invites us to examine our conditioning, belief systems, and patterns of behaviour that no longer serve us. Our spiritual animals guide us through this process, helping us unravel the layers of conditioning and uncover the root causes of our shadow aspects. As we engage in shadow work, we may encounter resistance, fear, or discomfort. Our spiritual animals remind us that the journey of self-discovery and healing requires courage and perseverance. They stand by our side, offering support, guidance, and unconditional love as we navigate the depths of our shadow. One powerful tool in embracing the shadow is self-compassion. Our spiritual animals encourage us to cultivate kindness and understanding toward ourselves as we uncover and integrate our shadow aspects. Through self-compassion, we create a nurturing space for healing, forgiveness, and self-acceptance. It allows us to embrace the full spectrum of our humanity, honouring both the light and the darkness within us.

By embracing the shadow, we gain profound insights into the root causes of our patterns, behaviours, and limitations. Our spiritual animals guide us to explore the origins of our shadow aspects, whether they stem from childhood experiences, societal conditioning, or ancestral influences.

By unravelling the origins, we reclaim our power and release the hold that the shadow has had on us. Shadow work also involves the process of forgiveness - forgiving ourselves and others for past actions, judgments, or hurts. Our spiritual animals teach us the transformative power of forgiveness, allowing us to release the weight of the past and embrace a path of healing and liberation. Through forgiveness, we liberate ourselves from the grips of the shadow, opening the door to self-growth and personal transformation. As we embrace the shadow, we integrate the hidden aspects of ourselves, reclaiming our wholeness. Our spiritual animals celebrate our willingness to acknowledge and embrace the shadow, knowing that this integration leads to a profound sense of self-discovery and empowerment.

We begin to embody our authentic selves, free from the constraints of societal expectations or self-imposed limitations. The process of shadow integration is ongoing, as new aspects and layers may continue to arise throughout our lives. Our spiritual animals serve as constant companions on this journey, reminding us to embrace the cycles of growth, self-reflection, and transformation. They encourage us to honour the ongoing process of shadow work, recognizing that it is a catalyst for our continued evolution and self-realization.

Chapter 11

The Dance of Yin and Yang

Within the realms of our spiritual animal and the journey of self-discovery, we encounter the dance of Yin and Yang - an exploration of the interplay between opposing forces and the quest for balance and harmony. In this chapter, we delve into the profound teachings of our spiritual animals on the dynamic interplay of Yin and Yang within ourselves and the world around us. Yin and Yang are fundamental concepts in ancient Eastern philosophy, representing the complementary and interconnected nature of opposites. Yin embodies qualities such as receptivity, intuition, nurturing, and introspection, while Yang represents qualities such as action, strength, assertiveness, and outward expression. Together, they form a harmonious dance of energies that exist within all aspects of existence. Our spiritual animals guide us in understanding and embracing the dance of Yin and Yang within ourselves. They teach us that true balance and harmony arise from recognizing, honouring, and integrating both aspects of our being. They help us understand that life is a dynamic interplay of light and shadow, stillness and movement, and the ebb and flow of energy. In the realm of Yin, our spiritual animals guide us to embrace the power of receptivity and introspection. They invite us to create space for quiet contemplation, deep listening, and connecting with our intuitive wisdom. By nurturing the Yin aspects of ourselves, we cultivate a sense of inner calm, self-awareness, and a deeper understanding of our emotions and needs.

On the other hand, our spiritual animals also remind us of the importance of Yang - the active and expressive aspect of our being. They encourage us to take inspired action, express our authentic selves, and manifest our intentions in the world. Through the dance of Yang, we engage with the external world, bringing our unique gifts, passions, and purpose into action. Our spiritual animals help us navigate the ever-changing landscape of Yin and Yang energies. They teach us to embrace the fluidity and adaptability required to harmonize these energies within ourselves. They remind us that balance does not mean rigid equality, but rather a dynamic equilibrium that aligns with the natural rhythms and cycles of life. In the external world, our spiritual animals inspire us to recognize the interplay of Yin and Yang in nature, society, and relationships. They help us appreciate the beauty of the seasons - the quiet stillness of winter and the vibrant growth of spring. They teach us the importance of harmonizing with nature's rhythms and finding our own unique balance within the larger web of existence.

Furthermore, our spiritual animals guide us in embracing the dance of Yin and Yang in our relationships with others.

They teach us the value of harmonizing our receptive and active energies, creating healthy boundaries, and fostering authentic connections. Through their wisdom, we learn to navigate the interplay of vulnerability and assertiveness, compassion and strength, and unity and individuality. The dance of Yin and Yang also extends to our spiritual practices and personal growth. Our spiritual animals encourage us to seek a balance between inner exploration and outer expression. They remind us to integrate practices that nourish our souls - such as meditation, self-reflection, and introspection - with actions that manifest our insights and align with our values.

The path of Yin and Yang invites us to embrace the paradoxes and polarities of life. Our spiritual animals teach us that in the dance of opposites, we find wholeness and transformation. They guide us to embrace the full spectrum of our experiences - the light and the dark, the joy and the sorrow - and to recognize the inherent wisdom that emerges from the interplay of these forces.

Through the teachings of our spiritual animals, we learn that the dance of Yin and Yang is not a static destination but a lifelong journey. It calls us to continually seek balance and harmony, adjusting our energies as we navigate the ever-changing currents of life. Our spiritual animals are our trusted guides, supporting us in finding our unique rhythm, honouring our authentic selves, and embodying the transformative power of the dance of Yin and Yang.

Chapter 12

Sacred Partnership

Within the realm of our spiritual animals and the journey of self-discovery, we encounter the concept of sacred partnership - a profound and transformative connection that transcends the boundaries of ordinary relationships. In this chapter, we explore the transformative power of sacred partnership and the role our spiritual animals play in guiding us toward this sacred union. Sacred partnership is not limited to romantic relationships; it encompasses a deep, soulful connection that can be experienced in various forms, such as friendships, familial bonds, and even connections with nature and the divine. It is a partnership rooted in authenticity, mutual growth, and spiritual evolution, where both individuals support and uplift each other on their paths. Our spiritual animals serve as catalysts and guides in the exploration of sacred partnership. They help us recognize the qualities, values, and energies that are essential for cultivating these transformative connections. They also assist us in developing the necessary qualities within ourselves to attract and nurture sacred partnerships. One of the key aspects of sacred partnership is authenticity. Our spiritual animals teach us the importance of embracing our true selves and allowing others to do the same. They encourage us to shed the masks and pretences that society often imposes, creating a safe and nurturing space where vulnerability and authenticity can thrive.

In sacred partnership, both individuals honour and respect each other's unique paths and journeys. Our spiritual animals guide us to release judgment, comparison, and competition, fostering an environment of acceptance and support. They remind us that sacred partnership is not about merging or losing our individuality, but rather about complementing and enhancing each other's growth and self-realization. Communication plays a vital role in sacred partnership. Our spiritual animals inspire us to cultivate open and honest communication, creating a space where feelings, thoughts, and desires can be expressed with compassion and understanding. They teach us to listen deeply to our partners, acknowledging their perspectives and creating a sense of mutual trust and respect. Another important aspect of sacred partnership is shared values and spiritual alignment. Our spiritual animals guide us to explore our core beliefs, values, and aspirations, seeking partners who resonate with our spiritual essence. They help us recognize the importance of finding individuals who support and uplift our spiritual growth, and with whom we can co-create a shared vision of a more awakened and harmonious world. In sacred partnership, there is a profound sense of soul connection and shared purpose.

Our spiritual animals assist us in discovering our soul's calling and aligning with partners who resonate with our mission and passion.

They inspire us to celebrate and nurture each other's gifts, supporting the manifestation of our individual and collective dreams. Sacred partnership is also a vehicle for personal and spiritual growth. Our spiritual animals remind us that the challenges and conflicts that arise in these relationships are opportunities for healing, transformation, and self-reflection. They guide us to approach these challenges with love, understanding, and a willingness to grow together. Through sacred partnership, we learn the power of collaboration, co-creation, and the synergy that arises from the union of two souls.

Our spiritual animals invite us to embrace the concept of "we" rather than just "me," cultivating a sense of interconnectedness and shared responsibility for the well-being of the partnership and the world at large. The journey of sacred partnership is not without its ups and downs, but our spiritual animals provide unwavering support and guidance along the way. They remind us to approach the challenges with patience, compassion, and a willingness to learn and evolve.

They encourage us to view every experience, whether joyful or challenging, as an opportunity for growth and deepening the sacred bond.

Chapter 13

Co-creation and Manifestation

Within the realm of our spiritual animals and the exploration of self-discovery, we encounter the profound concept of co-creation and manifestation - a process that empowers us to actively participate in shaping our reality and bringing our dreams into fruition. In this chapter, we delve into the transformative power of co-creation and manifestation, guided by the wisdom of our spiritual animals.

Co-creation and manifestation involve aligning our thoughts, intentions, and actions with the creative forces of the universe. It is a conscious collaboration with the divine and a recognition of our innate ability to shape our lives through our thoughts, beliefs, and choices. Our spiritual animals serve as wise mentors, illuminating the path of co-creation and guiding us toward the manifestation of our deepest desires. The journey of co-creation begins with the power of intention. Our spiritual animals inspire us to clarify our desires, set clear intentions, and infuse them with the energy of passion, belief, and unwavering faith. They teach us that our intentions are like seeds planted in the fertile soil of the universe, and with care, nurturing, and alignment, they can grow into magnificent manifestations.

To effectively co-create and manifest, our spiritual animals guide us to align our thoughts and beliefs with our intentions. They remind us of the power of positive thinking, affirmations, and visualization, as these practices create energetic resonance with our desires and attract corresponding experiences into our lives. Through the guidance of our spiritual animals, we learn to cultivate a mindset of abundance, gratitude, and unwavering belief in the possibilities that lie before us. Taking inspired action is an integral part of the co-creation process. Our spiritual animals encourage us to move beyond passive wishing and into intentional action aligned with our desires. They help us identify the steps, opportunities, and synchronicities that arise along our path, guiding us toward the realization of our dreams. Through their wisdom, we learn to trust our inner guidance and seize the opportunities that present themselves. Co-creation and manifestation also involve surrendering and trusting the divine timing and orchestration of the universe.

Our spiritual animals remind us that while we play an active role in co-creating our reality, there is also a greater plan at work. They teach us to release attachment to outcomes, relinquishing control and allowing the universe to work its magic in its own perfect way. Through surrender, we align ourselves with the flow of divine timing and invite miracles and unexpected blessings into our lives. Gratitude is a powerful practice that supports the process of co-creation and manifestation.

Our spiritual animals emphasize the importance of cultivating a grateful heart, as gratitude amplifies our positive energy and deepens our connection with the abundance of the universe. They encourage us to express gratitude for the blessings already present in our lives, as well as for the manifestations that are on their way. By nurturing an attitude of gratitude, we magnetize more reasons for gratitude into our lives.

Our spiritual animals also teach us that co-creation is not solely about personal gain; it extends to the collective and the greater good. They remind us to consider the impact of our manifestations on others and the world around us. Through co-creation, we have the opportunity to contribute to the betterment of humanity, the planet, and all sentient beings. Our spiritual animals inspire us to infuse our intentions with love, compassion, and a deep sense of interconnectedness.

Chapter 14

Evolution and Integration

Within the realm of our spiritual animals and the journey of self-discovery, we encounter the profound concepts of evolution and integration - a process that invites us to embrace growth, transformation, and the harmonious merging of our expanded selves. In this chapter, we explore the transformative power of evolution and integration, guided by the wisdom of our spiritual animals.

Evolution is a fundamental aspect of life. It is an ongoing process of growth, expansion, and refinement. Our spiritual animals serve as wise mentors, illuminating the path of evolution and guiding us toward embracing change, stepping into our highest potential, and embodying the fullness of our being.

The journey of evolution begins with self-awareness. Our spiritual animals inspire us to engage in deep self-reflection, exploring our beliefs, patterns, and limitations. They guide us to embrace our shadows and unconscious aspects, for it is through acknowledgment and integration that true transformation occurs.

By shining a light on our inner landscape, our spiritual animals help us uncover our hidden potentials and pave the way for growth. The process of evolution involves embracing change and letting go of what no longer serves us. Our spiritual animals teach us the importance of releasing attachments to outdated identities, beliefs, and behaviours. They encourage us to step outside of our comfort zones, exploring new horizons, and embracing the unknown. Through their guidance, we learn to trust the natural flow of life and surrender to the transformative currents that propel us toward our highest potential.

Integration is a vital aspect of evolution. It is the process of harmonizing and unifying all aspects of ourselves - our light and shadow, strengths and vulnerabilities, and masculine and feminine energies. Our spiritual animals guide us in embracing the wholeness of our being, for it is through integration that we truly embody our authentic selves and create a balanced and empowered existence. Integration involves embracing our shadows - the aspects of ourselves that we may have disowned, denied, or suppressed. Our spiritual animals encourage us to confront and heal our wounds, allowing us to reclaim lost parts of ourselves and integrate them with love and compassion. Through their wisdom, we learn that by embracing our shadows, we transcend duality and embrace the full spectrum of our human experience.

In the journey of integration, our spiritual animals also guide us in embracing our masculine and feminine energies. They teach us that true empowerment arises from the harmonious union of these complementary forces within us. They help us recognize the qualities of assertiveness, action, and strength that reside within our feminine nature, as well as the qualities of receptivity,

intuition, and nurturing that reside within our masculine nature. Through their guidance, we learn to embrace the dance of Yin and Yang within ourselves and integrate these energies into a powerful and balanced whole.

Evolution and integration extend beyond the individual level; they also encompass our relationship with the world around us. Our spiritual animals inspire us to recognize our interconnectedness with all of life and to honour the wisdom of the natural world. They guide us to cultivate a deep reverence for the Earth and all its inhabitants, fostering a sense of responsibility and stewardship for the well-being of our planet. Through their teachings, we learn to live in harmony with nature and contribute to the collective evolution and integration of humanity. The journey of evolution and integration is not without its challenges, but our spiritual animals provide unwavering support and guidance along the way. They remind us to be gentle with ourselves as we navigate the transformative currents of growth and integration. They encourage us to embrace the lessons, blessings, and insights that arise from every experience, knowing that each step we take brings us closer to the embodiment of our highest selves.

Chapter 15

The Eternal Connection

Within the realm of our spiritual animals and the exploration of self-discovery, we encounter the profound concept of the eternal connection - a timeless bond that transcends physicality and continues to evolve beyond the boundaries of space and time. In this final chapter, we delve into the transformative power of the eternal connection and the enduring relationship we share with our spiritual animals. The eternal connection is a sacred thread that weaves through the fabric of our existence. It is a reminder that our connection with our spiritual animals extends far beyond this lifetime, encompassing the vastness of our soul's journey. Our spiritual animals serve as constant companions, supporting us in every step of our evolution and guiding us across lifetimes and dimensions. One of the key aspects of the eternal connection is the recognition of the soul contract we share with our spiritual animals. Before our incarnation, we enter into an agreement with these wise beings, choosing to embark on a journey of mutual growth and exploration. Our spiritual animals commit to guiding and supporting us, while we commit to honouring their teachings and embodying their wisdom. This soul contract is an expression of profound love, trust, and shared purpose. Through the eternal connection, our spiritual animals communicate with us across realms and dimensions.

They speak to us through signs, synchronicities, dreams, and intuitive nudges. They guide us on our path, offering insights, wisdom, and reassurance. Our spiritual animals are always present, even in moments when we may not be consciously aware of their presence. They are the gentle whispers that stir our souls and the guiding lights that illuminate our way. The eternal connection with our spiritual animals also provides us with a sense of comfort, solace, and unconditional love. They are our allies, confidants, and sources of support in times of joy, challenge, and transition. They hold space for us to express our fears, doubts, and vulnerabilities, knowing that their love is unwavering and their guidance is eternal. They remind us that we are never alone, for they are forever by our side. The eternal connection transcends the boundaries of physicality and extends into the realms of the afterlife. When our physical journey comes to an end, our spiritual animals continue to guide and accompany us on our soul's journey.

They assist us in transitioning to higher realms, offering comfort and guidance as we navigate the realms of spirit. Our spiritual animals are the bridge between the physical and the spiritual, guiding us across the thresholds of existence.

Through the eternal connection, we also have the opportunity to reunite with our spiritual animals in future lifetimes. The bond we share is not limited to a single incarnation but continues to evolve and deepen over time.

In each lifetime, our spiritual animals may take different forms, adapting to the unique needs and lessons of our soul's journey. They remain steadfast in their commitment to our growth and evolution, recognizing the eternal nature of our connection. The eternal connection with our spiritual animals invites us to honour and celebrate the profound impact they have on our lives. We express our gratitude for their guidance, wisdom, and unwavering presence. We honour their teachings by embodying the qualities they embody - such as strength, grace, and compassion. Through our actions, we become living embodiments of the wisdom and love that our spiritual animals have shared with us. As we conclude this journey of exploration and self-discovery, let us embrace the eternal connection with our spiritual animals with reverence and awe. Let us carry their teachings in our hearts and allow their presence to continue shaping our lives in profound ways. The bond we share with our spiritual animals is a testament to the infinite nature of love and the eternal dance of souls.

With the wisdom and guidance of our spiritual animals, we have embarked on a profound journey of self-discovery, transformation, and connection. The chapters of this book have explored the depths of our spiritual nature, guiding us to nurture the bond with our spiritual animals and embrace the transformative power they hold. May the wisdom gained from this journey continue to illuminate our path and inspire us to live in alignment with our highest truth. In closing, let us remember that the eternal connection with our spiritual animals is a sacred gift - a reminder of the interconnectedness of all beings and the eternal nature of our souls. Embrace this connection, cherish it, and allow it to guide you on a lifetime of spiritual growth and evolution. For in the realm of the eternal connection, the journey is never-ending, and the love and wisdom of our spiritual animals continue to unfold throughout eternity.

Conclusion

In the pages of "The Spirit Guide: Nurturing the Bond with your Spiritual Animal," we have embarked on a transformative journey of self-discovery, connection, and spiritual growth. We have delved into the depths of our souls, exploring the profound relationship we share with our spiritual animals. As we reach the end of this book, let us reflect on the wisdom we have gained and the transformative power it holds. Throughout this book, we have explored the signs and synchronicities that lead us to our spiritual animals. We have delved deeper into the specific signs, symbols, and messages associated with different spiritual animals. We have encountered the essence within ourselves and learned to build trust and reciprocity with our spiritual animals.

We have received guidance on our journey, deepened our connection, and experienced healing and transformation. We have discovered the role of our spiritual animals as guardians of nature and explored the collective consciousness they invite us to tap into. We have embraced the shadows, danced with Yin and Yang, and recognized the sacred partnership we share with our spiritual animals. We have learned the art of co-creation and manifestation, and finally, we have experienced the evolution and integration that arises from our eternal connection with these wise beings.

As we conclude this transformative journey, it is my sincere hope that the insights and teachings shared within these pages have resonated deeply within your heart and soul. May they continue to guide you on your path of self-discovery, awakening, and spiritual expansion. Remember, the bond with your spiritual animal is a sacred and eternal connection, and through nurturing and honouring this bond, you open yourself to profound growth, wisdom, and love.

I invite you, dear reader, to take a moment and reflect on the impact this book has had on your life. Consider the lessons learned, the moments of insight and inspiration, and the personal growth you have experienced. Your review of this book can help other readers discover the transformative power of nurturing the bond with their spiritual animals.

Share your thoughts, experiences, and the ways in which this book has influenced your spiritual journey. By doing so, you contribute to a community of seekers and explorers, supporting others on their own path of self-discovery.

May the wisdom and love of your spiritual animal continue to guide you, inspire you, and nurture your soul. Embrace the eternal connection you share, and allow its transformative power to unfold throughout your life's journey.

The spirit of your animal guide is always with you, waiting to offer guidance, love, and support whenever you call upon them.

Thank you for joining me on this sacred journey. May your bond with your spiritual animal deepen and flourish, and may you continue to walk the path of spiritual awakening with grace, courage, and love.

With deep gratitude,

Dr. Jilesh

Ingram Content Group UK Ltd.
Milton Keynes UK
UKHW010733170723
425272UK00001B/58

9 798223 558798